*Good sense and good manners.
An 1850 collection of good advice
for those wishing to appear
polite and well-bred at all times.*

The
ETIQUETTE
of
POLITENESS

Copper Beech Publishing

This edition first published in Great Britain by
Copper Beech Publishing Ltd
© Copper Beech Publishing Ltd 1995

ISBN 1-898617-07-4

A CIP catalogue record for this book is available from the British
Library.

Cover design: Geoff Gillard

Copper Beech Publishing Ltd
P.O. Box 159 East Grinstead
Sussex England RH19 4FS

"He is the very pineapple of politeness"

R B Sheridan

THE ETIQUETTE OF POLITENESS

CONTAINING

━━━◦◯◯◦━━━

HOW TO BEHAVE IN A ROOM

I have so much to include under this heading, that I scarcely know where to begin. Every movement, every look, and every inflection of tone, is more or less its constituent.

❦◦ - - ◦❦

*W*hen you happen to be standing in a room full of company, I should advise that you acquire the following method of:

- bending the arms so that they may repose a little forward, and so as to admit of the hands being easily clasped,
- one leg should be straight,
- the knee of the other slightly bent out,
- the body erect,
- the neck in its place,
- the head poised freely, without stiffness
- and the countenance expressing mildness and candour.

It is a mark of *extreme vulgarity:*

~ to thrust the hands into the breeches or waistcoat pockets; or

~ to warm one's back at the fire by raising the coat-flaps at an angle of forty-five degrees, while the rest of the company are *freezing.*

It is also both low and dangerous to *plop* down upon a chair, as if you had fallen from the house-top!

Some people have a very *ugly* habit of shouting - after five minutes silence, they will begin to converse again by an explosion!

I once saw a rather nervous lady thrown into hysterics by this sudden vociferation on the part of a gentleman who was sitting near her; and the impression it made upon her may be gathered from the fact that she *never* afterwards could look upon him without thinking of the 'Infernal machine.'

⊶⊜⊶

BEHAVIOUR AT THE DINNER-TABLE

*W*hen the servant announces 'Dinner!' to the company assembled in the waiting room, you must offer your arm to the lady with whom you have been conversing, and conduct her politely to the dining-room. The lady of the house, of course, goes first, and you and all the other couples 'follow the leader'.

❦∘ — ∘❧

In offering your arm, curve it outward, gracefully.

*O*nce, a tall, bony gentleman thrust out his elbow so suddenly (it was extremely sharp) - that it hit the lady in the side, cut open her silk dress, and caused her to scream violently, fearing she had been stabbed!

You see how dangerous these angular sort of movements are!

❦∘ — ∘❧

Seating

*I*n approaching a dinner-table, the ladies should always be permitted to seat themselves first; as to the particular part of the table *that* is always arranged by the host or his lady, whom in this respect you must always be solicitous to obey.

For my part, I like the French plan, of pinning the name of the guest to a napkin, which prevents all confusion.

Carving

*T*he art of carving is *a very necessary accomplishment*, but it can only be acquired by considerable practice. If, therefore, you should be ignorant of it, you must exercise a little tact, so as to procure some friend to be your substitute.

I once heard my friend somewhat wittily remark, that "a person who could not carve, was fit only for the *Sandwich* Islands."

Wine

*I*f you sit near the lady of the house, you must select an early period of the dinner at which to take wine with her.

Bowing your head, you should smile blandly, and half reaching to the decanter, utter in a soft tone,

"Shall I have the pleasure.....?"

She will bow politely in return; when you must half fill her glass and then your own; you then make another very slight obeisance before taking the glass to your lips.

This piece of etiquette being over, you are at liberty to *Hob and Nob* with any person at table, whether lady or gentleman; though if your sweetheart be there, you will in common gallantry select her first.

Anticipate Her Little Wants!

*I*nfinite care is requested on your part to prevent a lady from being necessitated to *ask* you for anything she may require at table.

You should anticipate all her little wants, less in words, than by a graceful flexibility of countenance and manner and without any interruption of the conversation you may be engaged in with her or others. Such conversation should be carried on in a voice of gentle and equable volume.

Forks

Silver forks are now common at every respectable table; and for my part, I cannot see how it is possible to eat a dinner comfortably without them. The *fingers* are the natural forks, and the best - but they are not fashionable, and next to them is the capacious fork of silver. You should divide your viands, and then use the fork exclusively, holding in the left hand a pellet of bread close to the plate, as a sort of assistance.

Napkins

*A*lways use the napkin before drinking wine and, if you are intent upon the latter with a lady opposite you, desire the gentleman next to her to fill her glass with simply "May I trouble you?"

Dessert

*W*hen the dessert appears, you should make an offer to the lady of the various kinds of fruit.

You should crack the nuts for her, and deposit the kernels on her plate.

Apples should be peeled and cut in four parts.

Oranges should be peeled and then cut in slices extremely thin, and powdered with white sugar.

It is impossible for a lady to eat an orange in any other way without stretching her mouth - spirting the juice over her dress and into other people's eyes - and staining her delicate skin the colour of a frog!

BEHAVIOUR AT A TEA-TABLE

$\mathcal{T}$he Tea-Table is the common rendezvous of the middle classes of society; and certainly a more simple or elegant meal than tea cannot be conceived. I should not have called it a 'meal' - it is a *refection*.

We meet together to sip an aromatic beverage, eat delicate cakes, and converse pleasantly. Half the company generally consists of ladies full of smiles! - how delightful!

Now, you must be on the *qui vive*, my friend, to supply the ladies with muffin, crumpet, toast, or bread and butter, by handing these delicacies round to them - (unless there be a servant in the room, waiting upon the company) .

Also, you must keep a sharp eye upon their cups, and the moment they are empty, convey them to the tea-table.

N.B. *Mention the name of the lady as you put her tea-cup and saucer down; and say (to the presiding lady) whether she will take more tea or not.*

Music

*M*usic very often comes after tea, when you must be ready to turn over the leaves of the music-book.

You must do this *without*:
- scrubbing your coat against the lady's cheek,
- knocking out her combs,
- smashing the candles,
- or cutting her finger-ends off, by leaning on the lid of the piano, and forcing it down with a crash!

You smile - but these things are often done, nevertheless!

If you take part in a duet, be sure your voice is in order, for I have known a whole company afflicted by a pain in the stomach, through some screech-owl of a fellow pretending to sing!

BEHAVIOUR AT A GARDEN-PARTY

Garden-parties are of every description, from the grand reception which finishes up with illuminations and dancing, to the quiet little afternoon spent in the modest grounds of some tiny suburban villa.

They are generally given in the months of July and August, when the flowers are in their fullest beauty.

In consequence of the variability of the English climate, it is impossible to send out the invitations very early, say more than a fortnight beforehand, and even then it is advisable to have the house prepared for emergencies, so that the entertainment may not be an entire fiasco in case of rain.

Invitations

Garden-party invitations are sent out on large invitation-cards, similar to those used for afternoon parties:

Mrs. Butterworth
At Home
from 4 to 8,

... or from 5 till 12, as the case may be, the nature of the entertainment being explained by the words "Garden-Party" being written in the right-hand corner of the card.

Answers are expected, as to all other invitations, so that the hostess may know how many she has to provide for. The family is usually scattered about the grounds, so as to be able to pay attention to the different guests.

The hostess or one of her daughters remains in the drawing-room, where the people are shown on entering. Some houses are so arranged that the hostess can receive her visitors upon a terrace leading into the garden, and this is pleasanter work than being tied to the house on a boiling summer's day.

The people who stay in the house to receive the visitors certainly have a very dull time of it, as they are completely cut off from the scene of action!

Strawberries

Tents are put up on the various lawns for refreshments, which consist of tea and coffee, and cakes and ices, but more especially fruit.

A garden-party is nothing without strawberries, and if much money is laid out on any part of the entertainment it should be in the department of fruit.

A pretty toilette

A garden-party presents a favourable opportunity for the display of a pretty toilette, and simplicity should be the prevailing idea of a dress, whether it be a costly one or otherwise.

Cool-looking muslins will have a happier effect than the most expensive material, and you should be careful that your dress does not look like an evening one done up to serve the day.

A hat always looks well at a garden-party, but bonnets are more suitable to married ladies.

With regard to the etiquette of politeness at a garden-party, always be careful to find your hostess both on entering and leaving, and for the rest, enjoy yourself and look as happy as possible!

HOW TO CHOOSE YOUR COMPANY

*F*ew people give themselves any trouble to think about this subject; and yet many may date all the disasters of their lives from having neglected it!

I am aware of the extreme difficulty which presents itself to a clear definition of what is, and what is *not* good company.

What is called the 'best company;' - that is, both as to the intellectual acquirements and to manners, is only to be found amongst the highest of our nobility; and as I write for the middle class of society, I need only adopt so much of the example of the former, as may be useful in promoting a greater degree of refinement.

Selecting our company

*T*he phrase 'selecting our company' is perhaps not the most appropriate; we are so much at the mercy of our circumstances, that it is almost impossible to select any particular portion of the community wherewith to associate, and exclude the rest; but in saying this, I do not mean to imply too great a liberality; the vicious, the low and vulgar, and the unprincipled, should be shunned as a pestilence.

The opposite extreme, also, is attended with little good, *frequent sacrifices to worldly advantage* and severe mortification; I mean an ambition to mix in society to which we do not belong - in which we hold, what our writers of the present day call 'a false position'.

The three distinctions of middle class in this country are outlined.

From these remarks you will easily discern the precise level to which you belong, and within that, you must practice the rules we shall hereafter lay down - modifying them agreeably to that good-sense, which I have no doubt distinguishes you.

❦⊙ - - ⊙❧

The Middle Class

There are three distinctions of middle class in this country, which comprise:

No 1

Those of the 'three' professions and persons holding tolerably high official situations

No 2

Bankers and Merchants

No 3

Shopkeepers

Persons having small independent incomes are sprinkled over these three classes according to their education.

I lay a particular stress upon this last observation, because (unless in the code of some Beau Nash of a country town) *birth* has really nothing to do with the social polity of the middle classes.

❦⊙ - - ⊙❧

BEHAVIOUR IN THE BALL-ROOM

A ball-room should, of course, exhibit the *ne plus ultra* of elegance and fashionable ease.

The least deviation from grace - the least want of polite attention is there remarked, and laid open to ridicule. I cannot therefore do better than recommend you to pay the most implicit regard to your dancing master.

For want of such advantages as he offers, I have known *young men tumble about like pigs let loose* - kicking the lady's shins, treading on their toes, tearing their dresses &c. &c!

Really, it is shocking to think that people will *dare* to *dance* (Dance, forsooth!) in a quadrille under such circumstances.

ODD TRICKS

*H*ow many people, in other respects extremely amiable, have certain unaccountable habits!

Very Bad Habits!

*S*ome are perpetually hitching up their clothes.
Others have a kind of snort like a young elephant.
Others again 'make faces' as if for a wager!
All very, *very* bad habits!

Not To Be Tolerated!

*P*utting the feet upon the fender,
clumsily knocking down the fire-irons.

Blowing the nose hard
without turning the head away.

Keeping your thumb and finger for any length of time in another person's snuff-box is highly improper!

As to seizing anyone by the button-hole, that is now exploded: I would as soon that a person seize me by the nose!

Eccentrics!

*I*t has been truly said, that an *absent* man is fit only for a desert: if so, an *eccentric* one is fit only for the company of wild beasts! Yet how many persons affect the latter odious distinction!

It is consolatory to know, that the persons of true talent or genius (for which the former are desirous to pass), are of all others the most exempt from that vanity which studies a part and acts a character! *Simplicity* is the invariable adjunct of a superior mind.

Laughter!

*M*oderate laughter is exhilarating; and I look upon those persons as ridiculously overnice, who would depress all enjoyment into a smile: at the same time it must be admitted, that a loud chuckle is a sure sign of excessive vulgarity.

❦◦--◦❧

*T*o sum up the hints under this division of my subject, I must caution all young people against trusting to those who would be thought *frank* and *honest*, because they can only be *rude*.

They talk of the 'noble bluntness of the Englishmen,' as if there was a virtue in brutality, but they are, in truth, the knaves they appear to condemn, a mixture of the bear and the tiger, against whom the barricades of prudence should always be firmly advanced.

❦◦--◦❧

ATTENTION

*T*he most lamentable fault of any man, whether it respects business or amusement, is the inability to command an easy yet intense observation of all that is going on about him.

Concentration of mind

*I*f he goes to a dinner party, that circumstance should, for the time, wholly absorb him. I do not merely mean the cutting up of viands and eating them, but a close attention to that infinite detail wherein consists the essence of politeness.

If he go to an assembly, the same concentration of mind should prevail; and yet in both cases he should be entirely what the French call *dégagée*, and what we imperfectly express by the word 'easy'.

It will therefore be obvious, how incessant should be our observation, so as to enable us to perform, in the most agreeable manner to ourselves and others, those minor duties which our situation in society requires of us.

Never forget that celebrated aphorism of Dr Johnson,

"That which you would do with ease,
you must learn to do with diligence!"

CONVERSATION

*B*efore you can converse effectually, or in a manner agreeable to yourself and others, you must have acquired a control over your voice, so as to moderate it at will.

A Train of Thought

*I*t is well not to introduce a topic abruptly, but to communicate a train of thought to the persons with whom you converse, and so bring the subject you intend to descant upon gradually before them.

In this way you will give them a better opportunity of expressing their own opinion; and if your companion be a lady you should rather be an attentive listener, than a talker.

You should, if possible, know as much of hers or his, or the company's connections, as not to introduce any remark that may give pain.

A Narrow Mind

*I*t is at all times wise to avoid general reflections; such for instance, as are condemnatory of lawyers, doctors, or parsons, or of particular trades; besides, that nothing more clearly betrays a narrow mind.

Long Speeches

There are some persons who are extremely fond of making long speeches, which they have probably studied before-hand.

They no doubt think themselves vastly admired; but they are mistaken. It is a shocking interruption of the rights of society, and they are universally voted as Bores.

Of the two I would almost rather be drowned in a tub, than in a deluge of words!

Story-telling

Story-telling is also very dangerous ground, and requires considerable discretion in the person using it. But, because others are injudicious, it follows not that you should be rude; in all such dilemmas you must exercise a gentle and christian forbearance.

Dead Languages

*T*here are some, who, when they hear a word wrongly pronounced, immediately set the person aright: this is very faulty, and in fact, nothing more than the vanity of a petty triumph. Of a character analogous to this, is the desire to be thought learned, by making use of quotations from Latin or Greek. Why resuscitate these ghosts of the dead languages, when our own language, with the very occasional admixture of a living word from the French or Italian, is competent to every phrase of sentiment?

I always suspect a man who quotes to be a schoolmaster, who forgets that he may also be a *gentleman!*

Argument

*F*or my part, I like argument, when it is maintained with the most perfect temper; but the moment it becomes heated, I leave it to those who prefer noise to truth.

Puns

*I*n the present day, puns are much in vogue; and I am extremely sorry for it: I think them only fit for the *parterre* of a Yankey theatre! They are Goths that overrun the empire of conversation to lay it to ruins!

The Utmost Modesty!

*A*s a general rule, it is well not to interrupt those who are talking to you and if you feel yourself obliged to contradict, do so with the *utmost* modesty.

Humour

*H*umour is another thing; - when it does not descend into burlesque, it is always pleasant, and wit, moderately exercised, is delightful.

Scandal

*O*ne of the most prominent and detestable vices of the ages, is *scandal*.

Permit me amiable reader, to implore your abstinence from this most unchristian practice; look into yourself impartially. Are you so much purer than those around you that you can dare to be censorious?

I can assure you also that clothed in this *assassin-guise*, your own character suffers in the opinion of your hearers, infinitely more than you are aware of!

Satirical Jokes, Mimicry and Sneering

*S*atirical jokes, mimicry and sneering are all of the most unenviable distinctions; they betray a hollowness of the heart.

A merely mysterious man is generally a fool. And a man who introduces himself and his domestic affairs upon the tapis, is little better!

Egotism

*I*n truth egotism, which is frequently mistaken for generous openness, is nothing more than an excess of overweening vanity, surely there is something better to talk about than ourselves!

A person who has acquired a tolerable knowledge of the world, sees at a glance the kind of company he is in, and he adapts his conversation accordingly, and whether it be important or trifling, the atmosphere in which he moves (with more or less of sunshine), is a serious and dignified cheerfulness.

Small-talk

*A*s to *small-talk*, I am happy to say that it is now-a-days held in utter disrepute; what is it but another name for idiotic twaddle? The French word *badinage* means something very distinct, and something infinitely charming by the graceful playfulness wherewith it touches upon topic after topic; but it can only be acquired by the habit of mixing freely with polite and cultivated society.

I will conclude this part of my subject by enjoining you to pay an unswerving attention to the persons who address you, and to look them in the face, not staringly, but with earnestness.

-⊷⚊◉⚌⊶-

ADVICE TO YOUNG LADIES ON THE
ART OF PLEASING

Of the two, it is much less necessary to instruct *young ladies* in the science of being agreeable, than young persons of the other sex. They are early - very early - taught that not only their reception in society, but their establishment in life, must depend almost wholly upon the graces of manner; and they are therefore doubly assiduous to please!

Self-control

*Th*e habit of *self-control,* with a view to procure the good opinion of others, - and particularly of the sex for which they were born to be companions - becomes habitual to them.

Still, there are many degrees of excellence! - and from one who has seen and noted carefully the shades of good breeding, both in this country and in countries where it has arrived at a greater maturity, a few observations will not be inapt.

Music and drawing

As every young lady learns to dance as a matter of course, I have nothing to say on the subject of a graceful carriage; in fact, it is very rarely that we see an awkward girl, and, excepting in the wilds of Ireland, I should conjecture that a romp or hoyden was not to be had for love or money, and would be very dearly purchased for either!

I cannot agree with some of our more severe essayists, in condemning the time which is spent in accomplishing young ladies in music and drawing.

The former is so charming in company, and the latter is so beguiling as a *passe-temps* at home (where they are much confined!), that I deem them indispensable.

But I do think that the mental culture to be derived from books is much neglected, and that a good solemn system of instruction is in a majority of instances, never even made a subject of inquiry.

Permit me, therefore, you who have daughters to educate, a word of serious counsel.

Teach them to Think!

*T*each them to think before you crowd their young minds with tasks that, in a month after, become obsolete, or rather an addition to the chaos which your ill-judged plan may have generated: do this, and select books for them, such as combine amusement and instruction.

By conversing on the matters which these books treat of, you will improve their memories, correct deficiencies in pronunciation and utterance, and induct them into the art of conversation.

So far, therefore, we will suppose much achieved, and that the young lady being introduced pretty generally into society, goes on sensibly improving in all the attributes of manner; - now she may - I shall startle you gentle reader, - also be unconsciously declining into one of the most repulsive habits which can characterize her sex - she may be growing *Affected!*

Affectation

Of all things in the world, my dear lady, let not this disqualification be laid to your charge; and believe me, that it is much easier to be natural in all you say or do, than to be constrained in the hopes of captivating.

Whispering

$There$ is a fault, nay it is a downright cruelty - of which many young ladies are guilty in company - that of *whispering among themselves* at the expense of the male portion of the little community, or apparently so.

The act itself may be harmless or invidious; but it is always a fraud upon those present; it is a direct infringement of the laws of politeness.

Envy

$Envy$ is justly called a hag; for how can those, who *attach importance to themselves* only in as far as they may be useful and agreeable to others, indulge envy?

Cards

No young lady should sit down to whist or chess; they are what may be called *'cast-iron games'* and have a tendency to indurate the feelings.

A round-game, cribbage, or backgammon, are admirable, for they do not banish cheerfulness and pleasantry.

Awkwardness

*H*owever a young lady may walk into a room, or dance at a ball, she has sometimes a lolloping way of bending forward when she is seated; and for my life I cannot in my own mind dissever the idea of such a person from a Slattern.

A Slattern

If she *be* this last, she is to be pitied indeed! No habit grows more rapidly, - or becomes more eventually ruinous.

If she have this character at thirteen years of age, she will at thirty be a burthen to all who have the misfortune to be allied to her!

Amiability

*I*f amiability be valuable to man in his intercourse with the world, it is absolutely essential to *woman*!

The range of good qualities which it supposes is very extensive; it wholly banishes the most odious blot upon her sex, called '*satire*' with its attendant '*sneers,*' uncharitable constructions and vituperations.

Scandal

*S*candal is so prevalent, both in towns and villages, that its existence has been deemed of little moment, and *why?* Because not one half of it is believed.

Does then the other half inflict no injury upon the libelled? Let us even suppose it does not. Is it not a habit which has a tendency to blight in the bud all those virtuous and christian feelings, which can alone smooth the way to that better world wherein our pilgrimage will, we hope terminate.

A Shrew

I must candidly confess that I have never seen a *shrew*.
To be sure, I am not married, which may in some
measure account for the fact; but there is something so
exceedingly absurd in woman's taking pains to create misery
for herself, that I cannot help thinking the race has well nigh
disappeared!

A Blue-Stocking

*T*he age in which we live being distinctly that of *good
sense*, I am also sceptical as to the existence of *blue-stockings*.
If a lady be well-informed, she is only one among
millions equally so; and if she have learning or science, she
keeps it to herself, or shows it only in the works wherewith
she may favour the public.

Beauty

If you are *beautiful,* be not vain of the distinction; remember what Addison says, that "beauty may make virtue more intrinsically excellent;" but it may also, my fair and lovely auditress, make a way to undermine the purity of your soul, and overthrow the fabric of happiness!

If any man deliberately *flatter* you, deem it an insult, and politely but coldly request him to desist!

He has plainly a design, alike dishonourable to both, but of which *you* alone may be the repentant and outcast sufferer!

As to that lighter species of praise, which may spring from good-will, you will know how to separate it from the former.

Vanity - Dress

Vanity may also be directed to *Dress* - and though not equally fatal, it leads to many ill consequences.

In truth, *dress*, as a passion, may grow like any other, and be the destruction of a husband's quiet. It may also, by its train of coincident expenses, ruin his prospects, and bring a family to poverty and wretchedness!

My dear lady, you will know the value of a guinea, when you have to *borrow* it!

In dress, a young lady should be chiefly remarked for *neatness*. On the Continent, so particular are parents in this respect, that their daughters (unmarried) are not permitted to wear any ornament; and the same rule prevails in high life among ourselves.

Cleanliness

As to cleanliness, I will only briefly remark, that the word *lady* is entirely inapplicable to any one who may be deficient in this virtue!

Religion - Marriage

*C*herish religion - not as an austere ceremony - but as a sentiment.

It will be your best guide in that which is frequently a rock to the young, in the passion of Love. It will teach you rightly to reflect; it will instruct you in patient obedience to your parents, and it will show you how shameful and inappropriate to the good is coquetry!

Finally, it will conduct you, with the best hopes of happiness, to that state which is naturally the anxious object of a woman's contemplations, and on which her happiness hereafter, (so linked are the affections to the virtues) mainly depends - need I say, that I allude to marriage?

Humility

*I*n order not to be shunned and hated by your companions, you will of course avoid an *authoritative manner*, or the aiming at superiority.

Reflect on the perpetual lessons of humility. There is no more eminently beautiful quality in women than humility combined with simplicity of deportment.

Time

$\mathcal{W}$hen I reflect on the value of *time*, I cannot help feeling astonished at the trifling, the frivolous unsteadiness which marks the lives of many.

'Take care of the minutes'

- divide your days into portions, and occupy each strictly as you have planned, whether in your studies or your amusement, by which means you will give a zest to both; and be careful that the latter do in no case gain the preponderance!

Good Sense and Good Manners

Ladies should bear in mind that no beauty has
any charm equal to the inward one of the mind,
and that a gracefulness in their manners
is much more engaging
than that of their person.

Meekness and modesty
are true and lasting ornaments.

A sweet temper has a soothing influence
over the minds of a whole family
where it is found in the wife and mother.

Good manners and propriety of deportment
should be the practice of our lives,
both in our most important duties
and in the trifling enjoyments of our lightest hours.

Good Sense and Good Manners

The over-doing of politeness
is as rude and disagreeable
as its neglect.

Do not reserve good manners for special occasions,
but be polite and well-bred at all times.

THE QUALITIES NECESSARY IN A GENTLEMAN

Truth

As confidence is, as it were, the key-stone of society, it must be evident that prevarication in any shape must have a tendency to disturb it; and that *lying* must destroy it altogether.

The man who tells a lie to hide a fault, is a mean and skulking coward, and he who tells one in order to perpetrate an injury is a scoundrel.

There is another class of men, who make a sinner of the memory, and take all opportunities of retailing exaggerated statements of their own doings.

There are vain men, weak and silly withal, who desire to be famous even at the expense of truth.

They little dream how soon they are found out; and how absurd a figure they cut!

These persons are extremely tenacious of their own property; that is, *their own lies,* and you cannot more surely make such a one your enemy than by adopting a story of his as your own.

They put me in mind of the unfortunate gentleman who fancied he had swallowed St Paul's, and went about in fear and trembling lest any one should swallow *him!*

Truth only can carry you through the world respected and beloved by all.

Sobriety

A debauched life is fruitful in ills to the body and the mind.

The monitor, Conscience, is not to be lulled, let the mere man of pleasure assert what he may; and a broken down constitution and a wasted fortune are poor returns for what was once deemed pleasure, but is passed away for ever! Under these circumstances, no person can keep his place in society, and therefore he ceases to be a gentleman!

Amusements

*T*hese are, in a great measure, indicatory of the gentleman or the blackguard; be therefore careful in their selection.

All amusements that require out-door exercise are particularly to be recommended, such as fishing, shooting, walking, riding on horse-back &c. But there is no amusement with a greater recommendation than dancing.

There are various other amusements a gentleman may enjoy; common prudence will teach you what to avoid, your good sense and natural taste will dictate what to enjoy, recollecting, that giddy mirth and frivolous nonsense are alike ungentlemanly.

Cleanliness

A gentleman should be *exquisitely clean*, both in his dress and person.

His linen should be without a stain. He should, at least *once a week*, resort to one of the numerous baths in the metropolis.

In *shaving*, I recommend his attention to the precepts of a celebrated cutler in the Strand.

Absence of Cant

Cant expressions are an indubitable mark of vulgarity.

Dignity &c

Dignity of men, and spirit to repel injuries, are essential to a gentleman, and are very distinct from pride, which is shocking and repulsive at all times.

Gentleness

Gentleness is not incompatible with the former qualities, and is always captivating.

Let it not, however, sink into imbecile softness, fawning or flattery or you will descend inevitably below the standard I have proposed.

Diligence

This is the road to success - and I am persuaded there would be few blockheads in the world if men were more generally diligent.

It is astonishing how much we might acquire or perform in the hours that are devoted to listlessness.

Duty

*W*hatever may be the routine which in our peculiar situation it comprises, *duty* must either be performed with diligence - or be a mere apology!

Good Sense and Good Manners

Let not your manners be too familiar,
instead of getting you respected, they will
bring you into contempt.

Let nothing but illness or urgent business prevent your
keeping an engagement.

Always adapt yourself to the manners of
any company you may be thrown into,
so long as they do not militate against your principles.

Pay a proper deference to your superiors, whether in
circumstances, education or age.

Good Sense and Good Manners

It is not polite to repeat a story
unless you are certain it is correct.

Remember that true politeness and
a strict attention to etiquette
is the only certain and correct indication
of good breeding.

Other books in this series:

THE ETIQUETTE OF AN ENGLISH TEA
How to serve a perfect English afternoon tea;
tea traditions, superstitions, recipes - including
how to read your fortune in the
tea-leaves afterwards.

THE ETIQUETTE OF LOVE AND COURTSHIP
The old-fashioned art of wooing.
Advice from the 1850s.

ETIQUETTE FOR GENTLEMEN
Rules for good conduct for the gentleman
in every woman's life!

For your free catalogue containing these and other
Copper Beech Gift Books, write to:

Copper Beech Publishing Ltd
P O Box 159 East Grinstead Sussex England RH19 4FS

*Copper Beech Gift Books
are designed and printed
in Great Britain*